Jesus my Friend

Joe and Kristina Inzerillo

Jesus is my closest friend,
He lives inside my heart.
He may not be visible,
But we're never apart.

When I rest my head at night,
I think about my day.
It is to Jesus that I speak,
Of gratitude I pray.

What a lovely day I've had,
With so much love and light.
It is Jesus that I thank,
For all that has gone right.

And when the day was less than great,
I feel that Jesus knows,
Of all my special gifts and thoughts.
For me such love He shows.

I know tomorrow brings more joy,
For Jesus is my friend.
In all the ways a friend is good,
His blessings never end.

If ever I am feeling lonely,
I simply say a prayer.
I think of my friend Jesus,
Remembering He's there.

If ever I am feeling down,
I reach my heart in hand.
And this is something I can feel,
That He's always around.

Thank you Jesus for this day,
And all the love You gave me.
I had a lot of fun with You,
So glad You followed my way.

And so I ask,
Dear Jesus,
Will You and I always be friends?
And will I always find You?

The answer came without a voice.
No words,
No sight,
Just feeling.
As sure as I can hear my heart,
The answer's always in me.

For Jesus put me on this Earth,
So He could have a friend.
And all this time I searched for Him,
Turns out He searched for me.

Amen

Jesus My Friend

Copyright © 2019 by Joe Inzerillo and Kristina Inzerillo

www.kristinainzerillo.com

All rights reserved. No part of this publication may be reproduced, distributed, or transmitted in any form or by any means, including photocopying, recording, or other electronic or mechanical methods, without the prior written permission of the author, except in the case of brief quotations embodied in critical reviews and certain other non-commercial uses permitted by copyright law.

Tellwell Talent
www.tellwell.ca

ISBN
978-1-7340735-1-5 (Hardcover)
978-1-7340735-0-8 (Paperback)

www.ingramcontent.com/pod-product-compliance
Lightning Source LLC
LaVergne TN
LVHW072015060526
838200LV00059B/4679